BIGHORN SHEEP

Published by Smart Apple Media
1980 Lookout Drive, North Mankato, MN 56003

Design and Production by The Design Lab/Kathy Petelinsek

Photographs by Robert McCaw, Joe McDonald, Tom Stack & Associates
(Erwin & Peggy Bauer, W. Perry Conway, Jeff Foott, Sharon Gerig, Thomas Kitchin,
Joe McDonald, Mark Newman, Doug Sokell, David & Tess Young)

Library of Congress Cataloging-in-Publication Data
Frisch, Aaron.
Bighorn Sheep / Aaron Frisch.
p. cm. — (Northern trek)
ISBN 1-58340-016-8
1. Bighorn Sheep—Juvenile literature. [1. Bighorn sheep. 2. Sheep. I. Title. II. Series.

QL737.U53 F753   2001
599.649'7—dc21   00-050488

First Edition

2   4   6   8   9   7   5   3   1

NORTHERN TREK

BIGHORN SHEEP

WRITTEN BY AARON FRISCH

SMART APPLE MEDIA

*According to one Native American legend, the Great Spirit arranged
a marriage between the bison and the eagle, and the offspring from
this marriage was the bighorn sheep. With its stocky build and
ability to climb steep cliffs nearly as fast as many animals can run,
the Rocky Mountain bighorn does almost seem to be a small buffalo
with wings. Although many animals live in the Rocky Mountains,
none live at a higher elevation than the bighorn.*

BIGHORN SHEEP

(*Ovis canadensis*) are powerfully built animals. Males, called rams, stand about three and a half feet (1.1 m) tall at the shoulder and can weigh more than 300 pounds (136 kg). Females, called ewes, are a little shorter and generally weigh around 160 pounds (73 kg).

With their short, muscular legs, bighorn sheep are perfectly built for walking on uneven ground. Their **cloven hooves** are sharp-edged and flexible, with a soft, leathery pad in the middle. This unique hoof structure gives the bighorn excellent traction and helps to absorb the impact of long jumps or drops.

The male bighorn's most distinctive feature is its awesome set of horns, which sweeps backward in a curve. While ewes have only small spikes, a big ram's massive horns may measure 44 inches (1.1 m) or more along the outer curve. By the time the ram is seven or eight years old, its horns will have developed a

---

Bighorn rams can live 20 years, and ewes can live 24 years. Few bighorns, however, live much past 10 years in the wild.

full curl—that is, the tips will have reached the base of the horns in a full circle.

Around the end of October, bighorn rams begin to get restless. Mating season has begun, and only the strongest males will earn the right to produce offspring. To earn this right, rams engage in spectacular battles. When two competing rams square off, they slowly walk away from each other. When they are about 50 feet (15 m) apart, they whirl around and charge at full speed. As they meet, the rams lower their heads and slam their horns together with a thunderous crack that can be heard up to two miles (3.2 km) away.

During battles, intelligent rams position themselves uphill from their opponents and use gravity to speed their charges.

A limited number of bighorn hunting licenses are sold each year, and only mature rams—males whose horns are at least three-fourths curls—are legal game in most areas.

The force of these bone-jarring collisions is tremendous. The blow often dazes the rams, who may stand nose to nose for a few moments with their eyes glazed over. They then slowly back away before turning to charge once again. The battle may rage for hours (the longest fight ever witnessed lasted 25 hours) before one ram indicates surrender by walking away.

Despite the great violence with which battling bighorns collide, injuries are rare. This is

Although battle injuries are rare, a bighorn ram may suffer broken ribs when a third male charges into the fight.

Bighorns naturally adjust the size of their herds to the size and quality of the habitat available. If the area's food supply is poor, few lambs are born into the herd.

because bighorn rams have developed an unusual skull and neck structure. A unique hinge-joint connects the skull to the bighorn's strong backbone, and the bone covering the top of the animal's skull is double-layered. Bighorns also have thick muscles and extra-strong **tendons** in their necks, which help to absorb the blows.

For most of the year, bighorn rams roam in bachelor herds of up to 15 animals, while the ewes and young sheep live in bands that are twice as large. Only during the mating season do the herds come together. Females prefer to mate with large-horned rams—which tend to be the most successful fighters—so most of the lambs born in a herd are the offspring of the same dominant male.

After mating, ewes are pregnant for about six months. In the spring, just before they are ready to give birth, the ewes climb high into the mountains and find a safe, secluded place to give birth. A newborn sheep weighs about as much as a human baby and can follow its mother around within hours. After several weeks, lambs form little groups of their own and return to their mothers only periodically to nurse.

Bighorn sheep live throughout much of the Rockies. They are one of the few North American mammals that can live high in the mountains year-round. Bighorns move to several different feeding

Bighorn lambs are often looked after by an "aunt" sheep, an old ewe that can no longer reproduce.

areas throughout the year—higher ranges in the summer and lower valleys in the winter. They feed on a wide range of vegetation that includes **lichen**, flowers, tree buds, **sedges**, and berries.

Bighorns always graze close to steep rocky slopes that they can use as escape routes if **predators** attack. The sheep are wary and have excellent vision. If they spot a predator nearby, bighorns will sprint to the nearest cliffs, hitting speeds of up to 35 miles (56 km) per hour. They will then bound up the cliffs in a series of scrambling leaps.

This escape strategy allows bighorns to elude almost any enemy on foot. If a predator attacks at a higher elevation, the sheep can flee down cliffs with equal ease, dropping more than 10 feet (3 m) from one tiny ledge to the next. The only predator capable of occasionally catching adult bighorns during their bounding escapes is the mountain lion.

Bighorn sheep have no upper teeth in the front of their mouths, so they eat by chewing food between their lower teeth and upper gums.

Bighorns can walk across high mountain ledges as narrow as two inches (5 cm). They are hard prey to catch in such areas. Scientists studying bighorn sheep have even seen rams knock coyotes over cliffs with their horns.

In addition to mountain lions, the bighorn's wild enemies include wolves, coyotes, and eagles, but these are normally a threat only to young sheep. Humans also kill a number of bighorn sheep every year. In fact, a large bighorn ram is widely considered the greatest hunting trophy in North America.

Bighorn sheep came to North America two to three million years ago by crossing a land bridge that joined what are now Siberia and Alaska. Bighorns thrived until as late as 1850, when at least one million of them roamed the Rocky Mountains. Around that time, workers laying railroad tracks across the western half of the United States told stories of being watched by huge herds of curious bighorns perched on nearby ledges and cliffs.

Those railroads brought dramatic changes to

the bighorn's way of life. Settlers moved west and built cattle and sheep ranches, pushing the bighorns higher into the mountains. Although bighorns were not slaughtered the way bison were, they soon faced an equally deadly threat: disease. Strange new illnesses and **parasites** spread from domestic sheep and cattle to the wild mountain sheep, and bighorns began to die off rapidly. By the 1930s, the bighorn was nearly extinct.

Although their population has since increased, bighorns have not bounced back the way other species decimated by humans in the 1800s have. Only about 35,000 Rocky Mountain bighorns exist today, and about 25,000 of their close relatives, the desert bighorns, live in the southwestern United States. Only with human cooperation will the majestic bighorn continue to reign as king of the mountains.

Unlike a deer fawn, a bighorn lamb doesn't hide while its mother feeds, but follows her everywhere while she grazes.

BECAUSE THEY LIVE

in such remote areas, and because their population is rather small, bighorns are not commonly seen in the wild by the general public. National parks throughout the Rocky Mountains offer the best opportunities to see these sheep in their natural environment. Many parks provide specific information on where visitors can see bighorns. Listed here are parks that feature bighorn habitat and public access. Remember that wild animals are unpredictable and can be dangerous if approached. The best way to view wildlife is from a respectful—and safe—distance.

JASPER NATIONAL PARK IN ALBERTA *This large Canadian park is home to many lofty mountain peaks and nearly 3,000 bighorns. Some of the best places to catch a glimpse of the wild sheep are along Highway 16 in the eastern part of the park and along the Icefields Parkway at Tangle Falls.*

ROCKY MOUNTAIN NATIONAL PARK IN COLORADO *This popular national park features the highest highway in the world—Trail Ridge Road. It also features a healthy bighorn population. The best place to see the animals is at Horseshoe Park near Sheep Lake. Visitors can often watch from the parking lot as bighorns are lured in by a natural mineral lick.*

YELLOWSTONE NATIONAL PARK IN WYOMING *This most famous of national parks includes an abundance of wildlife, including bighorns. Visitors may spot bighorn sheep along the road through the Gardner River Canyon and near Dunraven Pass on the Grand Loop Road.*

cloven hooves: *hooves that are divided into two parts*

lichen: *plants that grow on rocky ground in mountainous areas*

parasites: *organisms that live off other living things and often cause disease*

predators: *animals that kill other animals for food*

sedges: *grasslike plants that grow in marshes or near water holes*

tendons: *cords of tough tissue that connect muscles with bones or other muscles*